CREEPY TICKS

CREEPY BODY BITERS

Brynn Carroll

Gareth Stevens Publishing

Please visit our website, www.garethstevens.com. For a free color catalog of all our high-quality books, call toll free 1-800-542-2595 or fax 1-877-542-2596

Cataloging-in-Publication Data
Names: Carroll, Brynn.
Title: Creepy ticks / Brynn Carroll.
Description: Buffalo, NY : Gareth Stevens Publishing, 2027. | Series: Creepy body biters | Includes glossary and index.
Identifiers: ISBN 9781482479454 (pbk.) | ISBN 9781482479461 (library bound) | ISBN 9781482479478 (ebook)
Subjects: LCSH: Ticks--Juvenile literature. | Parasites--Juvenile literature
Classification: LCC QL458.C377 2027 | DDC 595.429--dc23

Portions of this work were originally authored by Lorraine Harrison and published as *Freaky Freeloaders: Bugs That Feed on People: Ticks*. All new material in this edition is authored by Brynn Carroll.

Published in 2027 by
Gareth Stevens Publishing
2544 Clinton Street
Buffalo, NY 14224

Designer: Beeline Media and Design, Inc.
Editor: Tricia Hoffman

Photo credits: Cover, p. 4 Soru Epotok/Shutterstock.com; cover, p. 1, 4, 6, 8, 10, 11, 12, 14, 16, 18, 20, 22, 23, 24 Vyacheslav Zolotarev/Shutterstock.com; cover, p. 1, 5, 8 nechaevkon/Shutterstock.com; p. 4 Photoongraphy/Shutterstock.com; p. 6 S.Zykov/Shutterstock.com; p. 9 Melnikov Dmitriy/Shutterstock.com; p. 11 BlueRingMedia/Shutterstock.com; p. 12 Eric Isselee/Shutterstock.com; p. 13 a_o_r/Shutterstock.com; p. 14 Heiko Barth/Shutterstock.com; p. 15 AnastasiaKopa/Shutterstock.com; p. 16 Danica Chang/Shutterstock.com; p. 17 Jay Ondreicka/Shutterstock.com; p. 18 New Africa/Shutterstock.com; p. 19 Vadym_Hunko/Shutterstock.com; p. 21 Juergen Faelchle/Shutterstock.com; p. 7, 20 Harry Collins Photography/Shutterstock.com

Printed in China

CPSIA compliance information: Batch #QS27GS: For further information contact Gareth Stevens, New York, New York at 1-800-542-2595.

CONTENTS

Words in the glossary appear in **bold** type the first time they are used in the text.

PARASITE!

Parasites probably sound scary to most people. They come in all shapes and sizes. If you spend a lot of time outdoors, you may have already come into contact with one!

Ticks are parasites. This means they live and feed on the body of another animal, which is called a host. Ticks feed on the blood of their hosts, including people. Ticks can sometimes pass deadly **diseases** to people and pets when they feed on them.

Ticks have eight legs and a flat, oval shaped-body. They are more closely related to spiders and scorpions than insects.

SMALL BITES

There are more than 800 species, or kinds, of ticks found around the world.

Don't let their tiny size fool you—ticks can be big pests!

COMMON TICKS

The black-legged tick is perhaps the most feared tick species in the United States. They are common, hard to spot, and can spread diseases. Black-legged ticks are commonly called deer ticks because deer are a popular host of these parasites. But they will also feed on dogs, cats, and even humans.

Black-legged ticks live throughout the United States. They live wherever you find deer and **rodents.**

SMALL BITES

Female black-legged ticks are larger than males. Females are about the size of a sesame seed. Males are dark brown, but females are red with black markings.

Adult black-legged ticks feed on large **mammals** like deer.

WAITING FOR THEIR MEAL

Ticks can not fly or jump. Instead, they crawl onto a host after waiting patiently for one to walk close by. This is called **questing**.

A tick waits with its lower legs holding on to leaves or tall grass. It reaches out its front legs, so it can quickly crawl onto a passing host. Then, it finds a feeding spot, cuts into the skin, and puts its feeding **tube** into the host. This tube helps hold the tick in place while it feeds.

SMALL BITES

Some ticks can make their host feel numb when they bite them. This means the host can't feel the tick on their skin.

Sometimes a tick can stay attached to its host for days.

THE LIFE OF A TICK

Ticks can live for up to three years. A tick's **life cycle** has four basic stages, or steps.

A tick starts its life as an egg. Then, a larva comes out of the egg and finds a host. Ticks must feed in order to move from one life cycle stage to the next. Most ticks like to have a different host at each stage.

At the end of its time as a larva, a tick molts, or sheds its skin. It then becomes a nymph, which is like a small adult tick. After the nymph feeds and molts again, it becomes an adult. A tick takes about two years to go from an egg to an adult.

SMALL BITES

Adult black-legged ticks can live for nearly a year without food or water.

Life Cycle of a Tick

EGG
- laid by female tick off the body of a host
- often found in piles of fallen leaves
- hatch after three to six weeks

ADULT
- females are about the size of a sesame seed; males are smaller
- feeds on larger mammals, such as dogs, deer, and people
- females die after laying up to 18,000 eggs; males die after mating

NYMPH
- about the size of a poppy seed
- has eight legs
- looks like dirt or a freckle on a person's skin
- feeds on mammals, birds, or lizards

LARVA
- the size of the period at the end of a sentence
- has six legs
- feeds on lizards or small mammals, such as mice

SPREADERS OF DISEASE

Ticks are known to spread illnesses through their bites. If a host has **bacteria** living in it that cause certain diseases, the tick can take that bacteria into its body along with the host's blood. Then, it can put the bacteria into its next host.

One disease spread by ticks is Lyme disease. More than 89,000 cases of Lyme disease were reported in the United States in 2023. Lyme disease is one of the fastest-growing diseases spread by parasites in the United States.

SMALL BITES

Ticks are noticeably bigger after feeding. They may be up to three times their original size. That's because their bodies are filled with their host's blood!

Ticks can pick up diseases, or sicknesses, during any stage of their life cycle in which they feed on a host.

SIGNS OF LYME DISEASE

Lyme disease can cause a **fever**, headache, and other pains within days of being bitten. People with Lyme disease can also get a rash—a group of red marks on the skin—that looks like a **bull's-eye**.

If Lyme disease goes untreated, a person could get very painful headaches, pain in their **joints**, changes in their heartbeat, and even brain problems such as short-term memory loss. Luckily, Lyme disease can be treated by a doctor. Sometimes the signs of the disease can even go away on their own.

SMALL BITES

Black-legged ticks can spread other diseases to people as well, and some of these diseases can be deadly.

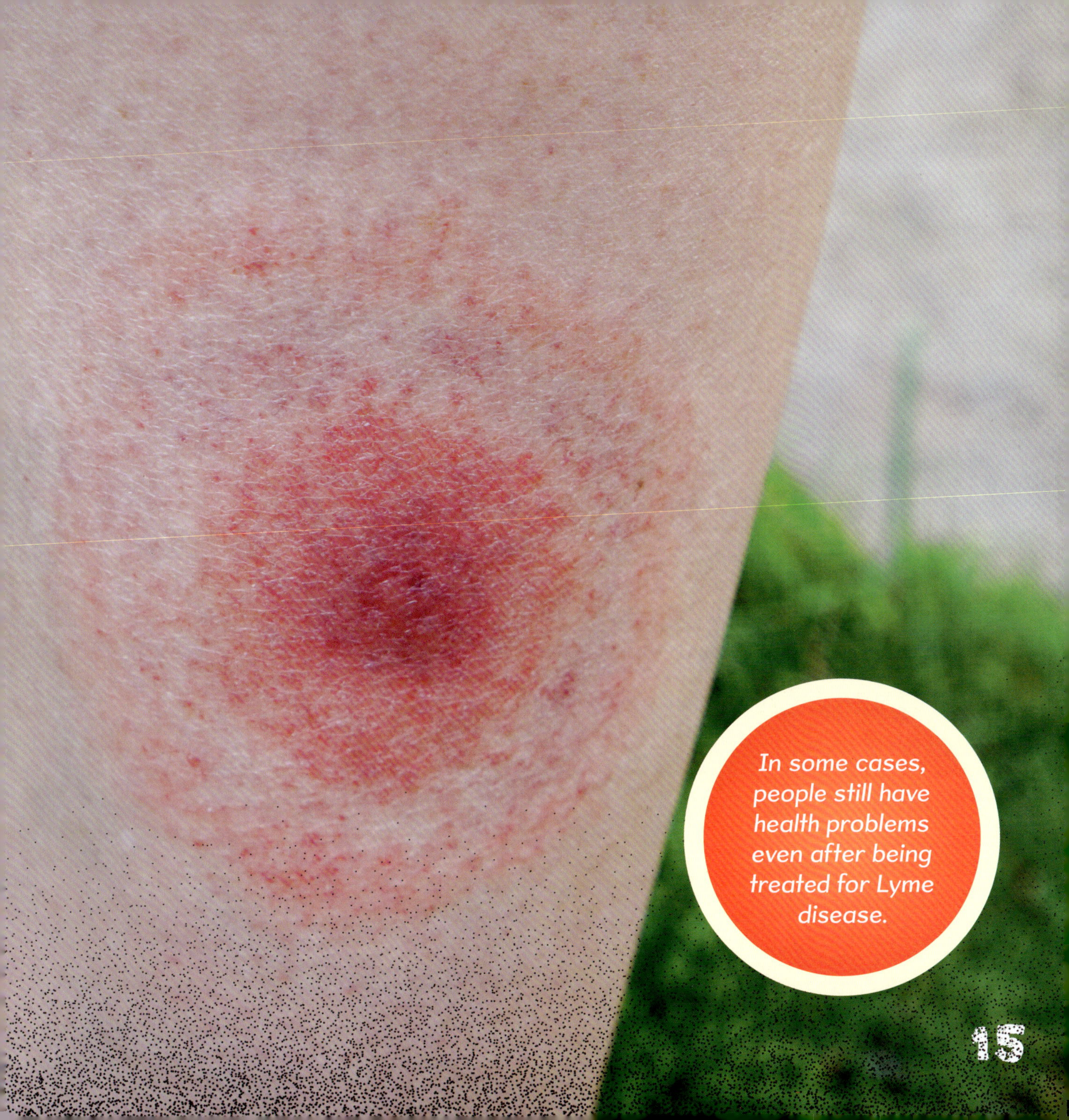

In some cases, people still have health problems even after being treated for Lyme disease.

MORE TICKS

The American dog tick can also spread disease, although it is less common than the black-legged tick. This tick is found throughout the country in areas east of the Rocky Mountains, but it's also found in smaller numbers in the western United States.

The American dog tick can spread a disease called Rocky Mountain spotted fever. This disease causes fever, headaches, body pains, and other health problems. It can be deadly. Luckily, most people recover with proper treatment.

The American dog tick is usually brown or reddish brown. It is larger than the black-legged tick.

STAY SAFE

If you go on a camping trip, you need to **protect** yourself against ticks. Stay in clear areas with less grass and overgrowth. Walk in the center of trails. Be careful when walking in wooded areas with tall grasses, especially in the spring and summer. This is when ticks are most active.

Wearing pants and long-sleeved shirts will help keep you safe. Tuck your pant legs into your socks to reduce the amount of skin that ticks can grab on to. However, ticks can also move from a person's clothing to their body. Put clothing in a hot dryer to kill ticks.

Don't assume that ticks only live in the woods. They can even live in your backyard, especially if it is overgrown!

Check your pets! Ticks can crawl onto people from the body of their pet. And dogs and cats can be hosts for ticks too.

HOW TO REMOVE A TICK

If you think a tick could have crawled on you, take a bath or shower as soon as you can. Then, check your body for ticks. If you do find a tick on your body, it's important to remove it as soon as possible. In most cases of Lyme disease, the tick must be on a person's skin for 24 to 48 hours before the bacteria that causes the sickness enters the body.

Use tweezers to take a tick off someone's body. Don't crush a tick with your fingers! A tick could still spread disease through a cut—even one that's too small for you to see.

SMALL BITES

Ticks may seem scary, but knowing more about these parasites helps us be better prepared to deal with them.

Pull upward with a steady motion so that the tick's feeding tube doesn't stay stuck in the skin.

GLOSSARY

bacteria: Living things made up of one cell, many of which cause sickness.

bull's-eye: The center of a target in sports such as archery, shooting, and darts.

diseases: Sicknesses.

fever: An increase in a person's usual body temperature.

joints: Points in an animal's body where two bones come together.

life cycle: The steps that a living thing goes through as it grows and dies.

mammals: Warm-blooded animals whose babies drink milk and whose body is covered with hair or fur.

protect: To keep safe.

questing: When a tick climbs to the top of a blade of grass and waits with its front legs outstretched.

rodents: Types of mammals that have long, sharp front teeth used for gnawing, such as rats, mice, and squirrels.

tube: A long, hollow object that can carry a liquid.

FACT CHECK

1. Ticks_______onto a host when it passes by.
   a. jump
   b. fly
   c. crawl

2. Ticks feed on_____.
   a. leaves
   b. blood
   c. flowers

3. True or false: Ticks only live in dense woods.
   a. true
   b. false

Answers: 1. c, 2. b, 3. b

ON THE INTERNET

Hey! A Tick Bit Me!
https://kidshealth.org/en/kids/tick.html
Learn important information about what a tick bite looks, what it feels like, and what to do about it.

Ticks
www.pestworld.org/pest-guide/stingingbiting-insects/blacklegged-deer-ticks/
Watch videos that teach you how to spot ticks and how to remove them.

Publisher's note to educators and parents: Our editors have carefully reviewed these websites to ensure that they are suitable for students. Many websites change frequently, however, and we cannot guarantee that a site's future contents will continue to meet our high standards of quality and educational value. Be advised that students should be closely supervised whenever they access the Internet.

INDEX